The LIVING WHEEL

A COMPLETE SYSTEM FOR

MANAGING CHANGE

Matthew Halligan

National Library of Australia
Cataloguing-in-Publication data:

The Living Wheel/White Light Publishing
ISBN: 978-0-6450180-7-3 (sc)
ISBN: 978-0-6450180-5-9 (e)

Dediction

My book is dedicated to those people who shared their personal pain and life experiences with me. They had a vital role acting as accommodation factors in the development and subsequent publication of the system.

To them I am truly grateful.

Acknowledgements

I want to express my gratitude to all those who have assisted me in the creation of the system. The support, help and belief, of Rhonda Steve, Pamela, and Mary F, in me and the system acted as contributing factors in the creation of the system and also in this publication. To my daughter Alexandra a constant friend during my years of continual change.

Everyone in their own way whether knowingly or unknowingly acted as accommodating factors in contributing to the creation and ongoing development of the system. A system intended and destined to be become a vital tool employed in the service of others.

To all of you. I am eternally grateful.

Matthew

Preface

Did you ever notice, become aware, or feel that something in your life was missing? A feeling of emptiness and /or of not feeling fulfilled? You have the material things and the latest electronic devices. You may even possess the luxury of employment in these uncertain times. Nonetheless this feeling is with you, and what's more, you're aware of its existence. This feeling has been with you for some time now, and it won't go away. It is constantly there in your awareness niggling away, like a reminder, waiting for you to respond. Perhaps the Livingwheel System for managing change can assist you in finding that which is missing.

Gratitude

A special word of thanks to my spiritual guide "Danielle", who has presented to me opportunities, her hand, wisdom and guidance, ensuring the creation of the Livingwheel System and this book in the service of others.

Namasté

Contents

The Theory

The Livingwheel System for managing change revolves around the premise that the universe offers gateways to us by way of our personal life experiences, which contribute to the process of restoration, balance and realignment in our lives.

These personal life experiences and/or synchronistic events are a communication to us and act as accommodating factors while assisting us in learning why we resist or embrace the process of change, thus allowing us to transcend and rise to a higher level of consciousness/awareness.

This new awareness is part of a process, reconnecting us with our true selves in remembering that which we have forgotten: our connectedness to all things and our true life's purpose. Simplified - a journey of the soul guided by synchronistic events or accommodating factors to arrive at its spiritual destination.

The Model

The model is constructed forming a 9 stage template tool, which is designed to convey the meaning of the theory. The operator can apply the template tool in their lives once instructed on how it works.

The Livingwheel template is a graphical or symbolic tool which describes and works with the theory, while identifying the stages of change throughout your personal journey.

About the Livingwheel©System

The Livingwheel System for managing change was inspired by events and experiences in my own life. I believe it assists with the restoration of realignment and balance in a person's life, while acknowledging that change happens to a person one step at a time and is unique to that person. It seems that the Livingwheel System for managing change is a universal tool unique to the person and their issue of concern. The Livingwheel System for managing change is a tool which can assist the person in the following ways:

Personal life issues, one step at a time.

Systemic approach while recognising that we live a life of choices.

Awareness to choices, based on the experience presented to us at any given time.

Assists the person uncover, discover and recover from old self-defeating negative patterns of behaviour, by raising personal awareness of the reasons why they choose to engage with, or resist the process of change and overcome self-sabotage.

Simplified - it's an introspective tool of creation with the understanding that the destruction of old thinking and behaviours accommodates the creation of newness.

What inspired the creation of the Livingwheel System?

It was events in my own life that inspired the creation of the Livingwheel System. The following are a few examples of how numeral 7 presented itself in my life.

My awareness of synchronistic events began in early 1992. For 25 years I had alcoholism, and my world revolved around alcohol. During that time I had an interest in numbers - I didn't know why, but I had. I remember as a child learning about the number 9. I had learned that you could multiply 9 by any other number and the result added together would always add to 9.

Here is an example of what I mean: 9x9 = 81, 8+1 = 9, or 9x4 = 36, 3+6 = 9. Try it yourself with any multiples of 9. This intrigued me, and I spent many hours playing with numbers. However later in life I became aware of numerology, the study and meaning of numbers and what they symbolise. I became aware of the number 7 and its prevalence in my life. The more I looked, the more I became aware of its presence and the fact that it always seemed to emerge into my awareness at a time of crisis or impending change. I began to believe that numeral 7 was in a symbolic way representing a compass, whose bearing was a clearly defined direction which I was to follow.

I had my own personal compass pointing me by way of direction and bearing along my life map. A journey which was to guide me along a pathway to an unknown destination. For me the scary bit was learning to trust as I was given the direction and bearing, but never the destination! It was like being on a mystery tour and only seeing the stops along the way while guessing at where the final destination might be.

I had to leave a world of control and predictability and venture into a world of unpredictability and uncertainty. This I felt could only be done by me learning to trust in my intuition, my beliefs and that strange feeling that events in my life were happening for a reason. I came to believe that numeral 7 was a communication from the universe to me by way of its appearance in my life, and more so, could only be interpreted by me. A key to unlock a door or a code which I had to decipher on a journey inwards of self-discovery.

Its presence in my life intrigued me. It seemed to be almost everywhere but I didn't understand why. However, intuitively I did know it had a meaning, a symbolic and special meaning. To me, it was more than just a coincidence. It seemed to have a purposeful and meaningful connection with me and events in my life.

When I tried to explain its occurrence to other people I was ridiculed and told I had an obsession. Perhaps I did, but thank God I didn't pay any heed or attention to them. I eventually realised I was trying to explain something deeply intuitive and meaningful to me, to people who didn't have the same level of awareness. I trusted in myself and continued with my observations as my awareness grew of its existence.

I was born on 23rd February 1953. In numerology this becomes $(2+3+2+1+9+5+3) = 25=2+5=7$. My father Matthew was 43 $(4+3=7)$ years of age when I was born and he died in 1980 at age 70. I am the 7th child in a family of 8 children, the second youngest, and my name Matthew contains 7 letters.

I was 7 years of age in 1960 $(1+9+6+0 =7)$ when my eldest brother emigrated to England. Earlier I spoke about my alcoholism: my first taste of alcohol was at the tender age of 16 $(1+6 =7)$. I had just finished school and began to work in a communications company in 1969 $(1+9+6+9=7)$. The same year (July 1969), my family moved to new accommodation.

The 14th of January 1994 was my first day of abstinence. It was on Monday 17th of January 1994 that I signed into a rehabilitation centre alone, frightened, fearful, and shaking from head to toe with delirium tremens also known as the DTs: the horrors or the shakes to address my alcoholism. After my initial assessment I was shown to my bedroom, which to my amazement – yes, you've probably guessed - was room number 7. Coincidentally or synchronistically, I was resident there for 43 nights to address those very issues which I had run away from for the previous 25 years.

My alcoholism was to last until January 1994, totalling 25 years. It had taken me that long to make that all-important cry for help. I could no longer go on the way I was, trying to control and beat the uncontrollable and unbeatable. I was beaten and I knew it. I surrendered, lost the battle but won what I have today at a huge personal expense.

My disease had finally caught up with me, and as the old saying in the East goes, "First the boy takes the drink, and then the drink takes the man". Looking back now at my experience in the rehabilitation centre I recognise that my experience was similar to that of a caterpillar who begins its life as an eating machine, finally retreating into a cocoon which allows a process of transformation to take place. This transformation or metamorphosis as it is known, allows change to take place by leaving the old behind and transforming into something new, colourful and beautiful, in a process of re-creation and the birth/emergence of a butterfly.

My time in treatment also gave me some new and necessary tools which would assist me with embracing my new life, including life without alcohol, my fears, joys, happiness, and most importantly, to assist with the restoration of balance and realignment in finding purpose and belonging in my life. With these restored I could be guided towards my divine mission and purpose, together with intuition and my personal and universal compass giving directions and communicating with me in a synchronistic and symbolic way.

Just like a seed which is placed into the earth to grow, it must decay first before the new seedling ascends through the darkness of the soil and towards the light. My days of living in the darkness were over. My life of alcoholism had decayed as I began the long and arduous journey of ascension towards and into the light. Upon reflection, my reconnection with myself and what is more important and essential was the reconnection with my Source from which I had been disconnected for the previous 25 years.

My reconnection came about on the third night of treatment. I was in my room number 7 when a light appeared outside of my bedroom door. This light was shining around the frame of the door and seeping in through the cracks and through the keyhole. I knew intuitively that I had to invite the light into the room and into me. At the time I was reading a book which contained a quote from the Bible stating, "If God is on my side, who can be against me"?

I placed the book on the bed and lay with my arms outstretched, palms pointing upwards, and said:

"I invite the light into my life, I invite the light into my life".

What happened then I can only describe as a powerful electric shock which I received in my navel and solar plexus. The force and power of the shock pushed and pinned me onto the bed on which I was lying. The light had re-entered my body, and me. I had been reconnected with my Source which replaced the darkness of my alcoholism, but not before I asked and was willing to accept the light into my life. The anxiety, dread, confusion, and fear I had been feeling up and until now was gone and replaced with an overall feeling of peace, contentment and calm. My spiritual ascension into the light of awareness had begun. I was no longer afraid. There is a Buddhist saying which says, "In the absence of light, there is darkness". Wouldn't you have imagined that as a keen photographer I would have known this?

You might be wondering what it was that brought me

into recovery. What was it that happened that caused me to cry for help? Well, it's very simple. My core fears were ones of rejection and abandonment. The very things I didn't want and feared experiencing, were the very things I was given to experience to allay my fears. They were my resistors in life. They were some of the unconscious and hidden anchors which contributed to, and acted as, a source of pain in my life. I was afraid of being alone and would do anything rather than experience it. I had to make the difficult and painful choice of leaving my family to connect with my cosmic family and find my true place of belonging and purpose.

The Livingwheel System for managing change was inspired by events in my own life. Those issues varied from relationship issues, unemployment issues, life changes, confidence building and increasing self-esteem. The Livingwheel System, I believe, can assist people who are experiencing recovery and maintaining that recovery from addiction, unemployment, personal assertiveness, accommodation change, product creation and personal change. A tool which assists the re-creation of the self. The Livingwheel System is simple to use yet powerful in use. It provides many applications for the person using it and is unique in its use for that person.

The Livingwheel System is a tool which assists in the process of change and maintaining that change. It helps identify the person's resistance or personal obstacles towards changing, acting as a tool of motivation towards a personal specified goal in a structured way. I believe the Livingwheel System can help identify and release the anchors (resistance) to change, promote personal progression (movement) towards embracing change and assist with the restoration of balance in the person's life. The Livingwheel System assists the person to embrace change while not changing the person. It can be incorporated on a one-to-one basis or as a group tool facilitated by the key worker, facilitator, mentor, etc.

The Livingwheel System pack consists of a Livingwheel template and workbook, which assists the person to remain focused thereby reducing the risk of self-defeating negative behaviours which can re-establish themselves if not closely monitored.

My experience of the Livingwheel System is that it can be applied to any issue which is the source of concern to the person as well as a tool of creation. It is a tool by which the person can identify and prioritise which issue they choose to engage with in "bite-sized" proportions at their own pace and time, promoting manageability and self-empowerment while reducing feelings of being overwhelmed.

Communication

We live in a world of communication from mobile phones to emails, internet and different types of media. All of which act by way of transmitting data for connecting and communicating with people. What connects them globally is a mesh of interconnectedness sometimes visible, sometimes invisible, called a network. Information and data being transmitted to us from the perimeters of space and beamed down to wherever the person might be. On another level we humans communicate to each other in some of the following ways: orally, body language, facial expressions, touch and eye contact, as well as pictures and drawing. The same principle applies in the animal kingdom. Whales communicate by sound waves, dogs by barking, birds by their chirruping, frogs, crickets and even to bees by way of their waggle dance (figure of 8, honeybee dance, Wikipedia) giving direction and the quantity of newly found nectar to worker bees in their colony.

I often visualise the conduit or thread between two people communicating is the attention given by both parties to what is being communicated. It's by paying attention we hear and absorb the other person's words.

In other words, we are listening. To put this in a symbolic sense, the cable which connects two people by phone could be seen as attention. It's the link between hearing and absorbing the other person's words.

As children we are often told "Pay attention". The reason for this is because we may miss the message of whatever it is we are supposed to hear or learn. The less distraction we have, the more we can pay attention. However in today's world of rush and importance to be busy, we seem to miss out on certain things and events which are being communicated to us.

Did you ever stand and look at the stars at night? Did they take your attention? Have you ever taken the time to look at the sun setting? The different designs on leaves and cobwebs left by frost, and/or listen to bird song in your back garden? Another example might be the sound of waves breaking on the shoreline, and what is more important, did you pay attention and listen? Paying attention is about giving time to the subject at hand so that we can answer based on what we have heard. This also includes our interpretation of what we have heard or the experience at hand.

What if the universe is having a conversation with us every day? Only in many ways it is the same conversation being repeated to us because we didn't pay attention, we weren't listening, so we didn't hear?

Just like if we didn't hear part of a conversation we ask the person to repeat themselves. It seems to me the universe does exactly the same thing. It repeats itself by offering us another chance to hear what it is communicating by way of our experiences and those experiences, albeit in different guises and shapes, return and revisit us so that our attention can be given to the lesson at hand.

The same would apply during a conversation. If we didn't understand what was being transmitted to us we would ask for clarity, thus enabling us to have a better understanding and interpretation of the message presented to us. The universe is working with us and not against us. There are other aspects of attention which I feel also play an important part in learning: intuition, clarity and interpretation.

Intuition

My internal, privately-owned navigation system. An internal compass which doesn't explain where it is I am going or where the path I am journeying will take me. It just points the way, giving me directions like a compass on a path which ultimately connects me with my destination.

In my experience, intuition is a "knowing" or "knowledge" From where it comes I do not know yet it comes as a vision or a picture sometimes, a glimpse of knowing that all the events which I am experiencing in the now are somehow linked to events in the future - not in an obvious way, yet there is connectedness nonetheless. For me, it's about having trust in myself and the self-belief that these events are all connected, while trusting in the fact that their connectedness have a purpose although not in a fully visible way. There is a hidden strand woven into each of the experiences which connects them altogether.

My experience of intuition is as though I get a vision or picture of the message, which I then piece together so that a clearer understanding of that which is being communicated can be interpreted by me and translated into my understanding. I believe my soul guides me on this path with synchronistic events as signposts which assist me stay on track for what it is I have to embrace. A connection to and with my soul. That part of me which is connected to all things in a permanent way. That part of me which is real and permanent compared to those things which are transient and impermanent.

An experience of knowing without knowing how I know until I begin to learn trust. Trusting that the information and wisdom given to me is a gift from the universe in assisting with, and helping me uncover, that which I have come here to do. An experience of trusting myself and my intuition as I journey this path. I believe all things happen for a purpose, but do I trust myself to believe and trust what I believe? I believe these synchronistic events and intuitive pictures are a communication from the universe to me during my life and I am willing to trust that that communication is for my benefit, guided by my soul, by way of communicating through intuition or knowing. A direct line of communication from my soul to me.

Absorb, Transform and Give Back - A principle of creation!

We live in a universe of interconnectedness, of which one of its laws is "By giving we receive". One of the natural processes by which I would symbolise this process is fog. After many days of rain which has had the effect of saturating the earth with water, eventually the sun

(accommodating factor) begins to shine and the earth is heated, giving back that which it has received, only this time, as water vapour or fog returning again to its Source creating new shapes as clouds. Another example of this principle can be seen in our relationship with the trees which surround us on a daily basis. Through the process of photosynthesis, light is absorbed from the sun and after a chemical process within the leaves, gives to us the necessary oxygen we require to breathe and sustain our lives. We breathe and absorb the oxygen while in return give to the trees the carbon dioxide which they require to sustain them. We have absorbed, transformed and created something new in return. We are engaged with, and are an integral part of, an interdependent relationship with our cosmic family and our environment. To put it another way, we are in the service of our cosmic family and have a place of belonging and purpose. In the examples given, there is an accommodating factor which assists in the transformation of change, but is not affected by the change. The essence of the accommodating factor remains the same. It is a process of creation.

A butterfly for example, by way of a process called Metamorphosis acting as a contributing and accommodating factor, transforms from caterpillar to butterfly in a cocoon, its natural process of change. Change being an inside job, the process of giving and receiving in this particular symbolic way is divided into three stages: absorption, transformation, and creation. At no point in the examples outlined is there resistance. Each of the examples given go with the natural flow of the experience in a process and purpose of creating something new. In other words, they "go with the flow" and give something new in the service of others in our cosmic family.

"A caterpillar is destined to become a butterfly through a process of embracing change"

Stage 1: Absorption

By applying this principle of change in our own lives, incorporating our new perception (when ready) enables us to view the experience as a gateway to change. Now that we are in a more conscious state of mind we see this experience as an opportunity rather than a hindrance, as we begin to embrace the process of change and create newness in our lives. Simplified, we accept and don't resist, and we have engaged with the experience.

Stage 2: Transformation

It's by accepting that the experience has meaning, and is given to us as a gateway for transformation or change, that we begin to understand we have learning which needs to take place. The meaning or learning is probably not obvious to us at the time. However, upon reflection the meaning may become more obvious and the learning more clear if we take time to listen to the conversation being communicated to us by way of the experience. We are now able to conclude that things happen for a reason. The reasons for which may not be clear at the time, but we gain clarity as we reflect on the experience and the associated factors which were the accommodating factors leading to transformation. We have absorbed, transformed and now it's time to give back, but not that which we have been given. We give back and contribute in a process of co-creation. Creating something new, in the service of our cosmic family.

Stage 3: Creation

We have reached the point of creation. We have created something new by way of absorption and transformation. We are conscious of our responses as they are actions which integrate into self-perpetuating cycles of cause and effect fuelled by our motives and intentions. When we reach this level of awareness, we possess a new set of tools which we can apply to our experiences. We are now consciously aware that each of our actions will cause a reaction. We are unsure of what that reaction or effect will be, although we are sure that our actions have created a reaction.

Belonging and purpose

Within our own family of origin to whom we are connected, we have a role and place of belonging. It seems to me that we follow this pattern in a place we call home where we feel a sense of belonging and purpose. In many ways we can observe this process within nature, for example, a seed whose purpose is to evolve through change and become a flower belongs in soil - a place of germination. Plankton belongs in the sea and is a source for the provision of food for aquatic animals as well as taking part in the process of creating oxygen. Trees belong in the earth and by way of a chemical process assisted by the sun called photosynthesis, receives carbon dioxide(CO_2) and releases oxygen(O), necessary to sustain life through their leaves. Earthworms belong in the earth where their activity includes the aeration and the mixing of soil while creating nutrients in the process, so vital for the replenishment of elements and the continual well-being of healthy soil.

The sun belongs in our solar system and is located 149,600,000km (Wikipedia) from the earth. It is our primary source of light, heat and energy. Again we see a place, belonging, purpose, and interdependence in our relationship with our cosmic family, our galaxy and ourselves. To me this system of connectedness and interdependence is not coincidental; quite the contrary. It suggests unity and balance orchestrated in a harmonious way in a system within which we are an integral part connected physically and spiritually in unison on a cosmic scale. As below so as above!

We don't have to look much further than our own bodies to see this principle at work. The vital components of the human body which contribute to a human being, on closer inspection, belong in certain areas and have a specific purpose and what's more, they belong and fit in their natural space. In many cases they have more than one purpose but the underpinning factor which connects them is the fact that they work in unison within an interdependent relationship with each other in a place of belonging and with purpose. At some point in life we begin to question the meaning of our lives. I believe this point is a gateway into realignment which has triggered us, leading into a greater understanding of our purpose, role and interconnectedness within our cosmic family. A state of awareness is made active assisting us into realignment, balance and a reconnection with our true self, a place from which we have drifted while never drifting from us. This reconnection helps us in recognising our true role and purpose by way of guiding us on a path to our divine mission. We begin to seek, perhaps unknown to us at the time, spirituality and the interconnectedness with the spirit of all things. We have awakened and are journeying into the light of awareness. We are on the path to finding our spirituality comprising of our true role and purpose, we are on the path to belonging.

Within the personnel section in most companies, each member of staff has a name, rank or grade and a staff number allocated to them at the commencement of their employment. The military for example, use name, rank, and serial number to identify each soldier. Other companies may have name, grade and staff number. There may also be different levels of the grade or rank of the position held. The two constants are the name and identifying number regardless of the organisation. I experienced this as an employee of a communications company where I held a position with ascending grades. The grade levels were dependent on the experience and proficiency of the employee in the particular area of their employment.

This process of identification as in the military (name, rank and serial number) I believe can be representative of a process in a symbolic way of identification in the universe. For example, my name is Matthew, my rank is light worker and my serial number is my date of birth (23/02/1953=7) given to me as I entered the earth plane. As I am no longer employed by the communications company, I am now an employee of a universal system (company) as a light worker (grade) and serial number (23/02/1953=7). The name of my employer is the universe. I have found my place of belonging and purpose working in the service of others so that they may awaken to their interconnectedness with and to all things to find their purpose and belonging within our cosmic family.

As below so as above! Divine timing or just synchronised coincidence?

We live in a world controlled by time. Time to me would be the distance between a cause and the associated effect. There is a time for planting seeds and a time for flowering. Even the tides both low and high are governed by the position of the moon at any given time during the day. There's a time from birth to death. A time from fertilisation to birth. A time for spring, summer, autumn and winter. A time for solar eclipse and lunar eclipse. There are 24 hours in our day, the time it takes for the earth to spin one complete turn on its own axis. It takes 365 days for the earth to orbit the sun. It takes approximately 28½ days for our moon to orbit our planet earth. Synchronised events seamlessly intertwined with all things exactly where they should be at any given time!

Just like the cycle of the seasons, when it's time for the leaves to fall from the trees in the autumn and regenerate themselves to create new buds and new growth in early spring. When we become aware of these cycles of events which present themselves to us on a daily basis in nature, we begin to learn the transience of all things. We know that the swallows leave Africa at a certain time and migrate to different countries arriving at a certain time. A perpetual cycle of change in a time completely different to, and not governed by, us mortals.

The same process can be witnessed regarding other breeds of birds who migrate from other countries at a specific time of the year to arrive at their new location to nest, give birth and return to their country of origin when their mission is completed. We could also compare these natural cycles relating to our families. When we reach an awareness that our time has come to move out of the family home, to obtain independent accommodation and create a life of our own. This migration from the home may vary from person to person, as they may feel fearful of leaving the security of the home and entering into the unknown. Perhaps it's for this reason they offer resistance and continue to stay in the known, rather than venture into the unknown, as they may have the perception of not being able to manage or care for themselves at a level which they have been used to up and until now.

People too enter into our lives at certain times, stay for a duration and then move on. Experiences follow the same pattern also. They arrive to us, we may engage or avoid them, but one thing is for sure, they don't last forever as all things are in a constant state of fluidity and change. It seems to me these experiences also have their own personal timing. There is also a time for separation. We often say we know it's "time to move on". This relates to our current employment which is no longer giving us the satisfaction that we require from a job. The same principle would apply to change of accommodation, for we no longer feel comfortable in our current surroundings and we look for something more affordable and even more comfortable.

We do the same with relationships. There comes a time when we need to move on from a relationship which has now become the source of our unhappiness. We may have lost the connection which was initially there. If so, we may also fear being alone, and should this be the case, we may resist moving on and choose to stay put. Even though the relationship is not in our best interests, it is serving us with purpose. We could apply the same principles to addiction. A relationship with a substance.

The same substance which we have, and most likely still are, using to take us away from the difficulties in dealing with life issues, now becomes a major life issue in itself. Now that we have become attached and dependent on it our life spirals downhill into addiction, chaos and unmanageability. A place we may not want to be in, but also may not want to leave. It's at some point within the cycle we consider seeking help as we can no longer function within the pain of addiction or a non-beneficial relationship with another person. In my experience, these patterns of events seem to come in cycles and have a natural cycle of a season and a reason.

We may also experience what I call the "Cosmic Shove" That critical event which motivates and drives us into action. An action that until now we did not need or want, as it would have meant changing something in our lives. We would have had to leave our comfort zone (albeit uncomfortable and destructive) to venture into the unknown, and what's more frightening, possibly alone!

The Livingwheel system for managing change acknowledges these patterns of events within the natural world. It also acknowledges that when changes take place in the natural world there seems to be very little resistance to that change. There seems to be a fluidity where the natural cycle of events are there to assist change, thereby recreating something new. It's as though there is a general acceptance and willingness to embrace change as part of a natural cycle within the natural world. Leaves for example, do not resist falling off branches in autumn. They do not cling on, as their natural time and work is complete on behalf of the life cycle of the tree. They now return to the soil from whence they came, as nutrients to decompose and become nutrients again, providing the tree with the necessary food it requires through the root system. Thus beginning the cycle of producing new buds and the formation of leaves the following spring. Simplified - they act for a season and a reason!

An experiential journey into belonging

A journey of the soul guided by synchronistic events or accommodating factors to arrive at its spiritual destination. I believe that all things are connected within our cosmic family and have a purpose and role. I also believe that we too are no different, as we have a purpose and a role within our cosmic family. I also believe that part of our mission in life is to reach an awareness of our interconnectedness, which is achieved as we journey the ladder of ascension to a higher vibrational level of awareness and understanding, accommodated by those experiences which we meet as we journey through life taking the form of initiation ceremonies.

I symbolise these experiences which we come across as experiential steps on a journey of ascension to a higher vibrational level of awareness. This could be symbolised in the physical realm as a train journey consisting of many stations on the track to its final destination. I believe the purpose of this journey of self-discovery is to consciously reconnect us with our higher self. A process containing and exposing our belonging and purpose, in other words, a purposeful adventure to uncover what it is we came here to do in this physical realm. A journey which helps us uncover our place of belonging and purpose within the universe, our cosmic family. Simplified - our experiences are initiation ceremonies which lead us into a higher vibrational level of awareness of our cosmic connectedness and divine purpose.

Clarity

When we don't quite understand what another person is saying or trying to communicate to us we look for clarity. We get clarity by way of asking what exactly they mean so that we can understand and interpret what they are communicating to us. We are now able to take the appropriate response or action as we have clarified what it is they are communicating to us. In other words, having sought clarity we now interpret what it is we need to do and take appropriate action.

We often use the phrase "The water is crystal clear", don't we? For me, this symbolises and translates into an image devoid of impurities, which if present, act as distractions affecting the transparency of the image. I am restricted in seeing through and beyond the current thought or vision. The same applies with embracing change. The importance of remaining steadfast and focused on the desired outcome devoid of distractions, your preferred choice will be confirmed to you on reflection. An explanation and description, in greater detail, can be found on page 40 "The Livingwheel System Explained".

Introduction to the Livingwheel System
A self-perpetuating tool of creation

As it has come from thought, and thought is of the essence. All things must come from essence by way of thought to materialise or become a creation in the physical realm.

essence = thought = creation = Livingwheel = recreation of self

Therefore the Livingwheel, I believe, is of the essence, as it has materialised and has been created by way of thought. The spirit lies within its structure, it is a "living tool". Simplified – it's a living tool and a tool for living

I believe the universe contains an intelligence. This intelligence connects and networks all things in the cosmos. In a symbolic way, it can be compared to and acts like an operating system similar to that found in every computer and computer network. This intelligence or operating system interconnects all things and flows through and from all things from its

Source. Another symbol of this concept can be found in the design of a cobweb with gossamer threads, acting as a network interconnecting and touching each strand while connected to its central core.

As we are co-creators, creating our own reality, what we create is made of and consists of the same intelligence. The Livingwheel was created from thought. So therefore the Livingwheel concept and construct is part of and contains the same intelligence. The Livingwheel has its own thought form as it symbolises the integration of this intelligence in its material shape, form and function, presenting itself in a symbolic and material way, originating from the Source of all things.

Therefore I ask, what is its thought form? Why has it come here in material manifestation? And what will it do in the service of others who operate the system? It seems to me the Livingwheel connects with the divine and acts as a tool assisting with recreating the self in a self-perpetuating way, assisting with the destruction of old patterns and belief systems while creating new ones, by way of awareness in the hands of the operator.

It is part of the spiritual and has its own role to play in people's lives. The Livingwheel has a function just like all other things created by man, who have connected with the universal intelligence as an expression of itself in the form of an idea or thought, in creating something of benefit in the service of mankind.

I believe the universal intelligence acts through us, as us, and by us. We are a channel or conduit from the spiritual to the material. The Livingwheel is a miniature universe for the process of creation, the natural process of evolution and the nature of all things. I also believe the Livingwheel has a place of belonging and purpose in people's lives, as with all things in the universe.

The Livingwheel is therefore a representative tool of transformation. It can assist people to embrace change who might otherwise feel stuck. I believe shock points or points of momentum are offered to us, which enable rotation and a continuous flow of revolution. Similar to a car tyre or a wheel which needs momentum in order to rotate from the thought Stage 1, with shock points at Stage 3 and Stage 6.

These shock points allow for momentum to take place in the cycle of recreating the self and promoting movement forward. A continuous perpetual tool of transformation to assist and enable the re-creation and renewal of self on a continuous basis, accommodated by our experiences. By bringing our unconscious patterns of behaviour into our consciousness, they can be exposed and changed. Thus assisting us in raising our personal awareness, leading to a greater understanding of who we are and more importantly, why we resist the process of change.

I believe that when we make this connection with ourselves, it helps with guiding us on our spiritual path so that we can experience a sense of purpose and belonging. As we become more awake and aware of our connection to and with all things in our cosmic family, we realise that we are no longer alone and release ourselves from our unconscious drivers and triggers of emotional dis-ease, with a conscious approach of engagement towards change to a place of belonging and purpose.

Our old behaviours and limiting beliefs gained by us by way of our life experiences and conditioning can paralyse us. However, we can free ourselves by using them to change our perceptions and beliefs. We must come to believe that the universe will always give us what we need, not necessarily what we want. In other words, the universe works with us, not against us.

We may not however, be aware of the meaning of the experience at the time. On reflection, we begin to see that things in life happen for a purpose and are for the best. We can achieve our divine purpose in the service of others while drawing us nearer to our Source, as it is by giving that we receive.

I believe we belong and are part of an overall living system, where we give carbon dioxide to the trees, so that they in return give us the necessary oxygen we need to survive.

We live in a system where the water from the sea evaporates by way of the sun, only to recreate itself as clouds, so that those clouds eventually return to us in the form of rain. The rain of course is necessary to replenish the earth, streams, and rivers so that we can avail of water, so vital to our existence. A continuous cycle of transformation, assisted by an accommodating factor or outside force.

We live in and are part of an inter-dependent system, where all things are connected, and are part of the universal intelligence from which we originated. We are in fact, the universe expressing itself through us, as us, and by us. We are a miniature universe, but most importantly, having access to the universal intelligence which is in abundance. It is an endless supply of creative energy which is at our disposal at all times, for our greater good.

The Livingwheel System explained

It's simple to use, yet powerful in its use. It is your own personal pattern identifier, with you as the inspector of your own behavioural patterns and a tool of re-creation.

The Livingwheel is divided into 3 triads:

Triad 1: Thought

Triad 2: Action

Triad 3: Transformation

Stage 1 - Issue of concern

Let's imagine some issue in your life which you are unhappy about. We will call this Stage 1 "The issue of concern". This issue is caused by someone or something, and is the cause of concern and disharmony in you. One way or another you are feeling unhappy, resulting in you experiencing disharmony and pain of some description as a result. However, as we are all uniquely different, the time frame in addressing these issues vary from person to person.

Ultimately your time for change is at a unique time for you. That is, up to the point when you decide you must do something about it. You are now very aware of its existence and the dis-ease and disharmony it is causing you in your life.

It might be a financial issue, it might be a relationship issue, an issue of accommodation, or addiction. Nonetheless, it is there and you know that you know it is there. The effects of this knowing is causing you dis-ease and disharmony in your life. These in fact, are the effects of the cause. It is in your awareness, and you are feeling the effects.

So what are you going to do about it?

Stage 2: Awareness

The effects of the issue of concern at Stage 1 have caused you to consider doing something. You are aware that you need to do something, but perhaps unaware of what it is you need to do, so you consider your options. You begin to verbalise your issue of concern. You talk about your relationship, your need for a bigger house or the need to change employment.

You might even pray for guidance or whatever it is that is necessary for you to cope with the issue, which is the source of dis-ease and disharmony which you are experiencing.

By doing the above, you create an effect. As mentioned earlier, the tide completes its cycle from high to low water in a time dependant on where the moon is in its orbit around the planet earth. You are sending out a message by way of verbal, psychological (thinking) vibrations. They, the vibrations take time! They have to be sent out, in order to return.

In many ways, it's like posting a letter to a friend. You write the letter, you address the letter to the recipient, you post the letter and wait for a reply.

So let's summarise what we have learnt so far.

Stage1: Something in your life is causing you disease, disharmony or discord, which is the issue of concern in your life right now.

Stage 2: The effects of the issue are the cause of your disharmony, which is now in your conscious awareness. This awareness causes you to consider your options, which may take some time as you may not be ready to make a choice. You have in some way sought help or guidance relative to your issue of concern. The vibrational frequency is out there, but you must wait on a reply, which is the effect.

This in turn will create a shock or synchronistic event to take place at Stage 3.

Stage 3 – Choices (Accommodating factor)

You receive a reply in due time of course. You are now working with divine timing and not your normal clock time. You see an advertisement for "relationship counselling" or you see or hear of a house for sale. One way or the other, the vibrations coming back to you by way of an outside force act as an accommodating factor with your actions/thoughts which you transmitted at Stage 2.

The universe has responded to your request. It is offering to you choices based on, and connected with, what you sent out at Stage 2.

So let's summarise the first triad which is: Thought.

Stage 1: You are experiencing an issue which is the cause of concern, dis-ease and disharmony in your life.

Stage 2: You become aware of its emotional effects on you.

Stage 3: An outside influence or shock point taking the form of a synchronistic event and/or an accommodating factor takes place in your life.

Now that you have arrived at Stage 3, you are aware of the new choices and accommodating factor/s which have entered your life. These choices and accommodating factors will assist you in embracing that all-important and badly needed change, which will begin the process for the restoration of balance and harmony in your life.

You now arrive and find yourself at Stage 4 in your process of personal change. It is here that you will resist or embrace those choices, which arrived into your life as accommodating factors at Stage 3. Usually at this stage you will resist or embrace the process of change. If you choose to resist, it may be due to the fact that as much as you may not want to be in the situation, (which is the cause of your dis-ease) you may not want to leave it, as you will have to take a leap of faith into an unknown world of unpredictability, uncertainty and even insecurity.

Stage 4: Resistance or Movement?

The effects of the accommodating factor or catalyst at Stage 3 (shock point), causes you to move forward or indeed resist the choices presented to you. Let's tease this out a little. If a car needs fuel to ignite its engine in order for it to move, I believe the same applies to us. In my experience, motivation is my own personal internal combustion engine, and just like any other engine, it needs to be fuelled by something. In this case our motivation (internal combustion engine) needs to be fuelled by need, want, desire, passion and determination. Any one of these emotions or a combination of these emotions are needed to ignite the internal combustion engine of motivation towards action.

No doubt you have experienced these emotions at various levels in the first "Triad" of issue, awareness and choices, but what about your "safety blanket"? What about your "comfort zone"? What about doubt? Uncertainty? Emotional attachment? Or even unpredictability, to mention but a few. Could it be that your beliefs, associated emotions and perceptions of the outcome act as resistors which prevent you from moving on and embracing your desired change?

I believe these beliefs and associated negative emotions can be overwhelming and can propel us back to Stage 1, where we re-experience the same issue of concern once more, and engage in a repetitive cycle of positive reinforcement of negative behaviours. This pattern of behaviour within the Livingwheel System is known as "The 1, 2, 3, 4 dance". This return to Stage 1 can be automatic as we secretly hope the situation or person will change. This belief, if real to you, may release you from having to do the hard work of engaging with changing yourself.

The provision of case histories at the rear of the book are designed to assist you, the reader, to identify the different stages of the Livingwheel System in other people's lives, thus allowing the reader to identify those behaviours with their own. In many cases, change only takes place when those motivational forces discussed earlier act as a fuel in order to ignite that internal combustion engine of motivation in you.

Change, in many cases, only takes place when there is a change of perception on your behalf. You come to the realisation, awareness or belief, that what you are going through has to be better than what you are leaving behind, even though you are travelling a path of uncertainty while journeying into the unknown.

Stage 5: Preparation

What were the accommodating factor/s which have occurred for you at Stage 3, the shock point? You have decided or chosen to remain at Stage 4, for whatever your reason. If this is the case, you will have returned to Stage 1 and you will have completed the Livingwheel "1, 2, 3, 4 dance".

You may have done this in the hope that someone or something will change, or for reasons that only you will know. You have remained at Stage 4 due to your fears, beliefs, and insecurities etc. You have resisted, and what you resist persists!

If however you have chosen to move forward, you have now reached the conclusion that you can no longer engage with or tolerate the disharmony you are experiencing. Something has driven or motivated you to embrace change in your current situation. You have done something different, and now you will receive something different in response.

You have in fact reached a personal milestone and need to be applauded. It took bravery, courage, stamina and even hope, that what you are doing is the right thing. You are beginning to trust, whereas up and until now, trusting may have been difficult for you. Your lack of trust and inability to change "you" have probably been a contributing factor to your resistance and doubt. So well done!

What is it you need to do now? Remember you're still at Stage 4 and still volatile in returning to Stage 1. But let's assume enough is enough and you are embracing this change for the better. You are about to jump the bridge from Stage 4 to Stage 5 and take a leap of faith into a world of the unknown. Scary but necessary!

At Stage 5, you researched and gathered the required tools, life skills, information, even support groups, to consolidate your decision in moving forward. Ask yourself, is there freedom in having experienced the fog of confusion at Stage 4?

Do you feel confident you are moving in the right direction? Does the decision feel right even though you might be feeling uncertain about what the future holds? Perhaps you may even ask yourself, could it be any worse than that which you have chosen to leave behind? So, what is it you need to do at this point? Here are a few examples:

If it is relating to new employment, you need to prepare and update your CV. You may need to research the new company and learn about what it is they actually do. What do they manufacture? What are their exports? The reason for this research is for you to gain knowledge and empower yourself with that knowledge.

When you post your CV wish it well, as the notice of the decision has come into you by way of the accommodating factor at Stage 3. It's important to remember only you have control over what it is you do, you have no control over the outcome. However, what you do affects the outcome in some way, as we are dealing and engaging with cause and effect.

It's preparation time! We will assume that you have prepared your CV. You have posted it to the relevant company and you have let it go! Which means you have handed over to a power greater than yourself. This in turn gives you time to research the company and its products etc. This research will be of benefit to you should your application be considered for the vacant position, while remembering you have no control over the outcome, only what you have submitted which affects the outcome.

Stage 6: Confirmation

Let's assume that all goes well for you. You're called for an interview, your research is done and you're feeling nervous yet confident that you have done all that it is you could have done. You have prepared well.

You attend the interview, all goes well and you feel a sense of relief. About seven days later you receive correspondence offering you the position. You feel excited and over the moon at the prospects of your new employment and you're going to accept it with great enthusiasm.

However, there is another side to Stage 6. Let's change the scenario a little. You have done as outlined above, prepared your CV, carried out the necessary research, prepared well, attended the interview, and awaited the results with expectation. You are now informed by correspondence that you were unsuccessful in your application. What a disappointment! How are you feeling now? What are the effects on you and what are you thinking?

Now that your application is unsuccessful, it's possible that you're experiencing uncertainty, disappointment, frustration and self-criticism. Is that the little voice in your head, full of negative self-chatter, and telling you all sorts of negative things?

But what if it were the case that there is a more suitable

position on the horizon for you, and that the universe was giving you a trial run in a lesson of trust? You see, you have made your choice to move at Stage 4 based on your experience at Stage 3, the accommodating factor.

So there is no need to go back to Stage 1. What you do is remain stable at Stage 4, and await a new accommodating factor or choice at Stage 3, which is your shock point and accommodating factor. You have already made up your mind that you want to move on, that much is already in place and has been created by you, based on your experience of this issue so far.

You continue to think about changing jobs, and the universe will respond and answer you at Stage 3. All you need to do is get out of the way and allow the process to take place. Remain positive in the knowledge that something better is on the way "in" for you.

When it does - and it will - you first prepare yourself for the new position and repeat steps 4 to 5. You submit your CV for the new position at Stage 6: Confirmation, working on the belief that you are powerless over the outcome, but not what you do, which affects the outcome. There is an old saying, "What's for you won't pass you by", which is a reminder to you that the universe works with you and not against you.

I believe one of the principal factors of synchronicity is the belief that the universal energy is working with you in a harmonious way. It's working with you to achieve the perfect outcome for your current situation. However, Rome wasn't built in a day and you are entering into a world of faith and trust. Patience is required so that you can achieve, in conjunction with the universe, your purpose and mission, which you have come to the earth plane to experience and complete.

You are no longer alone in your plight, you are consciously connected to the universe and on the path to embracing your divine mission and purpose, while more importantly, learning to trust. Another key factor in this is the belief that you are being guided, and that the universe will always provide for your needs and not your wants. As the saying goes, "If I have my needs, do I need my wants?"

You have now travelled the second triad (action), which consists of Resistance/Movement, Preparation and Confirmation.

Stage 7: Acceptance

Following on from the last example, the next stage on the Livingwheel is acceptance. I believe acceptance can be very difficult at times. It is about coming to terms with what has been offered or experienced by you, at any given time. It may not be what you want to accept. However, it may very well be what you need to accept, to allow your resistance, negative thoughts and emotions to dissipate for you to experience the gift in the presenting result.

Accepting that there is something better on the way requires belief, patience and trust, while being aware that you are not in control of the outcome of any situation. We only have control over the action we take which affects the outcome.

As the prayer suggests, "God grant me the serenity to accept the things I cannot change "today", the courage to change the things I can "today" and the wisdom to know the difference".

Our last example gave two attitudes towards acceptance:

1. Excitement, enthusiasm, elation, expectations, etc.

2. Disappointment, resentment, uncertainty, frustration, etc.

However, if you change your perception of the outcome while acknowledging the emotional reaction within yourself, you can change your perception to a more positive one, thereby changing the emotional effect to a more positive emotion. It is your perception of the event which affects your emotional response.

So, in the first case scenario you have been offered a position and have accepted it. This leads you to Stage 8, which is where you reflect on the events through Stages

1 to 6, which have brought you to acceptance at Stage 7.

You will find that by reflecting on the cyclical events with which you have engaged having left Stage 4, things begin to become clear (remembering that Stage 6 was also a shock point to move you forward to Stage 7 or help you to return to Stage 3). You waited here for yet another indicator or accommodating factor better favoured for you to achieve your desired outcome, while being mindful that learning is taking place at all stages of the Livingwheel System, enabling and accommodating your movement within the cycle of transformation. You are now at Stage 7 and move on to Stage 8 with acceptance.

Stage 8: Reflection

At Stage 8 you reflect on your process of change, and on the initial issue which presented itself to you at Stage 1- your issue of concern.

Reflecting on Stage 2 Awareness:

This includes your emotional dis-ease and how your issue of concern had affected you and the length of time you have endured your emotional disharmony.

Reflecting on Stage 3 Choices:

You reflect on the accommodating factor at Stage 3, the first shock point. You also reflect on what you were offered to facilitate change in your life, and what the defining factor/s or moment/s were which motivated you to move forward.

Reflecting on Stage 4 Resistance or Movement:

You reflect on what it was which prevented you from moving forward and embracing change. Was it doubt, uncertainty, fear, or dependency? Was it the belief that you couldn't do it? The fear of loss, abandonment or rejection? Did you fear that there was no going back? Did you at any point consider returning to Stage 1, and if so, why? What happened here at Stage 4 which motivated you to change and move across the bridge, to take that leap of faith from Stage 4 to Stage 5 preparation?

Reflecting on Stage 5 Preparation:

What preparation did you engage with in order to prepare yourself to allow and accept the process of change and move forward to Stage 6? What was needed to be done by you to prepare? What were you feeling? Did you have a sense or belief that you were doing the right thing? Did you experience a sense of freedom in leaving the old patterns of behaviour behind?

Reflecting on Stage 6 Confirmation:

What was it that happened which confirmed to you that you had made the right decision or choice?

In the case of the application for employment, if it were the case that you were unsuccessful, did you return to Stage 3 and await a new accommodating factor or synchronistic event? If so, in what form did it present itself to you when it happened?

Reflecting on Stage 7 Acceptance:

At this stage you just accept the outcome of Stage 6, plain and simple. Only this time with your new level of awareness, you know there is something better on the way in for you, in conjunction with Divine timing!

Reflecting on Stage 8 Reflection:

What conclusions did you arrive at? Looking back at the events and patterns of behaviours you had engaged with prior to now, did you become aware and learn what your personal resistance and anchors were, in your process of change? If so, they are now in your awareness, and you are mindful of them as possible unconscious anchors which may present themselves in the future. But you are aware of them now so that's half the battle. Below are some sayings which might help you at this stage of reflection:

"If you don't learn the lesson from the experience, you will re-experience the lesson".

(unknown).

"If you always do what you've always done, you will always get what you've always got".

Henry Ford (1863-1947).

"Life can only be understood backwards, but must be lived forwards".

SØren Kierkrgaard (1813-1855).

Stage 9: Completion

Over the past cyclical process, you have moved from an issue which has been of concern to you, while possibly experiencing emotional discord, disharmony, dis-ease, confusion, fear and doubt, to mention just a few.

Having engaged with the process of self-creation through the nine stages, how you are feeling right now? Is there a sense of achievement, freedom, movement, contentment, completion, or an improved sense of self-confidence and/or self- empowerment? If so congratulations and well done! Not only have you moved and engaged with the cycle of creation and personal change, but you have closed the door on one concerning aspect of your life. This issue of concern has possibly been with you for a prolonged period of time, having the effects of holding you back and anchored to the past.

Your behaviour up and until now has had a positive reinforcement of negative cycles of return, incorporating self-limiting belief systems and emotional responses and behaviours. These responses may have stemmed from your fear of rejection, abandonment and insecurity. More importantly, you have opened the door to a process of cyclical identification of what can be achieved, and it's only the beginning.

You may have completed a cycle of creation from one issue. However, it is only the beginning as you move forward, using this tool in your life to assist and motivate you as your own personal do- it-yourself coaching tool of self-introspection, while incorporating you as the inspector of your own behaviour. It's important to remember though, that even though you have travelled the 9 stages to completion, you actually begin a new journey, which is the effect of the collective and previous 9 stages. Collectively in their entirety they have become a cause, the corresponding effect of which has created a new and more desirable outcome. You now enter, and engage with, a cyclical process of renewal and re-creation in your life, at Stage 1.

The beginning
"Change is an inside job"

Livingwheel© System Template

This is the Livingwheel©System template for your personal use, as you are the operator of personal change in your life.

Case study for identification purposes

The purpose of the case study is to assist you, the reader, to identify the stages through which Richard has travelled on his journey to change, while assisting you in identifying the stages on your own journey of personal change.

Richard and the Livingwheel© System:

Case study 1

Richard, who is 50 years of age and employed for most of his working life, due to the economic downturn has been made redundant and is currently unemployed for the past two years. Richard is beginning to feel the effects of unemployment. He is experiencing lack of motivation, purpose and a sense of being left behind in his life. He is aware that the prospects of new employment seem to be travelling a downward slope because of his age and the current economic climate.

Richard fears that he may fall into depression as his self-esteem and self-confidence are being affected on a daily basis. Richard feels he has nothing to look forward to, and that his role in the family has been affected as he was once the main breadwinner and provider for the needs of his family and himself.

Richard decides at this point that he must do something which would assist with the restoration of wellness and balance in his life. Richard realises that he has choices. He can choose to remain in receipt of unemployment benefit or he can seek alternative employment of some description which would assist him with the process of restoring balance and wellness in his life. It is at this point Richard makes an appointment to visit the local employment agency.

Resulting from his visit to the local employment agency, he has received various job descriptions and requirements for vacancies in employment. However, Richard convinces himself that because of his age and lack of experience in the specific areas, it wasn't worth his while applying for any of the listed positions. He thinks it is unlikely that he would be successful, as he believes that his age and lack of experience in the specific areas would hinder his progress.

As a result of this negative self-chatter, Richard has now entered into, and engaged with, the 1, 2, 3, 4 dance. As a result of his self-chatter, loss of confidence, self-esteem and belief, Richard returns now to Stage 1 of the Livingwheel System whereby he experiences the same issue of concern as before. He remains unemployed with the risk of his fear of depression likely to increase.

On the other hand, Richard is willing to embrace change. He sees a vacancy which appeals to him. Richard is feeling excited at the prospect of new employment, which he hopes will assist him restore a badly needed sense of balance and wellness in his life. What is more important, Richard has broken the cycle of the 1, 2, 3, 4, dance. By embracing change, Richard is on a path which will help him reverse the effects of the negative emotions as he returns to a sense of meaning and worthwhileness in his life.

Richard has made his choice and prepares to engage with that choice. He does this by submitting the completed application form and forwarding it to the personnel section of the company. In the interim, Richard researches the company for relevant details, such as how long the company is in operation, details of imports and exports, and what the main manufacturing items of the company are. This information would be relevant and beneficial for Richard should he be called for interview in the coming weeks.

Not only did Richard receive confirmation from the company that they had received his application, they also, to his surprise, offered him a date for which to attend an interview. Richard is feeling excitement and nervousness at the thought of his impending interview, which by the date given is only ten working days away. However, with his preparation completed to the best of his ability he attends for an interview, with confidence, on the date assigned to him.

Richard attends for interview on the assigned date. He feels confident that he has done well and now anxiously awaits the outcome. Two weeks later Richard receives his long-awaited reply. He finds he was successful at his interview and was offered the vacant position. Richards's self-confidence as a result of this has increased, and is excited about the prospects of his new appointment. Richard contacts the company and duly informs them that he accepts the position. They in turn provide him with a date on which to begin his new employment. On the other hand, if Richard had received confirmation that his application or interview was unsuccessful, he would return to Stage 3 and engage with a new choice. In either case he has accepted the outcome whether his application was unsuccessful, or in this case, successful.

Richard now reflects on the process and his issue of concern and personal learning received from his experience. In particular, he reflects on the motivational, and/or accommodating factors which have assisted him in moving forward and embracing change. What is more important for Richard is that he reflects on those issues, which may have caused him to resist his process of change at Stage 4, thereby returning him to Stage 1 on the Livingwheel System.

Richard has travelled the nine stages of the Livingwheel System for managing change. He has travelled Triad 1 (thought). He was experiencing an issue of concern, became aware of its effects on him, and was offered choices. Richard has also travelled Triad 2 (action). He either moved with or resisted the choices offered to him. Next, he prepared himself in making a choice and awaited confirmation.

Richard has also travelled Triad 3

(transformation). He has accepted the outcome and reflected on his personal process and learning, while experiencing completion of this particular issue.

When Richard was unemployed he felt depressed, negative, useless, without purpose, and saw no hope for the future.

Having been introduced to, and incorporating the Livingwheel System in his life, he learned that he had choices that could change his situation and restore value, hope and purpose.

Case study for identification purposes

The purpose of the case study is to assist you, the reader, to identify the stages through which Joan has travelled on her journey to change, while assisting you in identifying the stages on your own journey of personal change.

Joan and the Livingwheel©System

Case study 2

Joan had been in secure employment for 10 years, or so

she thought. She was married with three small children, ranging in ages from 4 to 10 years. Her husband Tom enjoyed a position as an electrician who had plenty of work during the boom years and Celtic Tiger. However, when the construction industry collapsed, Tom found himself without a job and in receipt of unemployment benefits.

This issue took its toll on the family finances and more importantly, on their relationship. Tom, for the first time in many years, was without work and dependent on his wife Joan to meet the financial needs of the family. Joan too was feeling the strain. She had to keep the home, put food on the table, and meet with mortgage repayments and travelling costs, as they lived in the suburbs with her place of employment 20 miles from their home.

Initially they used some of their savings to meet with their financial commitments, such as school costs, doctor's appointments, etc. Over time their commitments began to erode their savings. These new pressures had the effects of triggering arguments and general unrest in their relationship. They reached a critical point and had to sell one of the cars to reduce some of their outgoings.

They cut back on their shopping, and the days of going to the cinema with the children were over as they could no longer afford the luxury. There were still school outings, books, swimming and football activities to be paid for, as well as birthdays and Christmas expenses.

Joan thought her employment was secure, although she worried constantly and feared what might happen should the company decide to relocate its business abroad in search of reduced running costs. Should this happen, it could affect Joan and ultimately lead to the loss of her job. In June 2011, the inevitable happened. A general meeting was called for the staff and they were informed that resulting in increased running costs, the management had no other choice but to reduce staff. Joan was devastated, her stress and anxiety increased, which began to cause an increase in her emotional difficulties. It wasn't long before the final decision was taken to relocate and Joan became another statistic of unemployment.

The situation was bad enough, but now it had gotten much worse. Both Joan and Tom, who was still unemployed, began to experience fear, uncertainty, insecurity and unmanageability. The bills had to be paid which they were trying to meet on reduced income, but what was going to happen now, to them and their children?

To keep some semblance of normality in the home they put on a brave face for the sake of the children. When the children left the house for school it was a different matter. They would buy the local newspaper and go on the web in search of positions vacant. They were becoming desperate and in receipt of phone calls and post demanding payments, as they were in debt and had fallen into arrears with the financial institutions.

They felt hopeless, and at one point considered emigrating just like many of their friends had done. One morning while listening to a radio programme, Joan heard of some charitable organisations and their work in the community. With great reluctancy Joan wrote a letter to the organisation requesting help, as winter was looming and she needed heating and fuel. In due time Joan received a reply from them and they agreed to meet with her.

The representatives agreed to help the family as much as they could to ease some of their difficulties. They also mentioned to Joan about the local money advice agency and the way they could assist her in managing on what little she had. Joan was very independent and was feeling a loss of dignity and self-respect as she felt she was begging for food to live and survive, barely existing.

Joan at this stage was attending her doctor for anxiety and stress which had increased and were causing difficulties for her. It was during one of these visits that she noticed a poster for a local agency which would assist her to manage financial issues. It was the same money advice service which had been mentioned to her by the charitable organisation, but she feared going to them in case she would be known.

She resisted contacting them and was feeling ashamed and embarrassed. She was also resisting contacting the financial institutions, as she feared losing her family home and becoming homeless.

The stress and anxiety was mounting and the pressure for money became greater. It wasn't until she received a letter from a solicitor concerning her mortgage arrears that she was pushed into doing something, quickly. She contacted the local money advice agency and made an appointment with them, although fear and embarrassment made her reluctant to go. Joan plucked her courage from somewhere and met with them on the date given.

As requested, Joan brought relevant documents and papers with proof of debts and arrears, as well as evidence of what she was receiving by way of unemployment benefit. She found the meeting very beneficial and the staff very friendly. They assisted her in creating a budget plan which would be put in place over a period of weeks, helping her keep track of household income and expenses.

Joan began learning to prioritise, while at the same time was made aware of various schemes which could be put in place by the financial institutions which would assist in addressing their mortgage concerns. The main concern was keeping a roof over their head and food on the table. She learned that the necessary forms and schemes by the financial institutions could be downloaded online, completed and returned to the financial institution for approval. This would take a couple of weeks before being approved and initiated.

However, with the support of the money advice agency she felt she was getting somewhere rather than ignoring the difficulties. She felt a sense of relief as it took bravery, courage and commitment in overcoming her fears to engage with and complete the process. Joan is now dealing with each financial issue in turn while prioritising their basic needs as a family such as food, clothing, electricity, life insurance, house insurance and fuel, etc.

However, even though she has engaged with her debts there is still a shortfall, and they are relying on some charitable organisations for assistance. Both Joan and Tom are still in the process of seeking full-time employment, but have been unsuccessful to date.

Joan's manageability of her issues have been further assisted after attending a workshop she saw advertised called the Livingwheel System for managing change. She now has a tool and system for dealing with issues of concern one step at a time, by way of prioritising and assisting her with the restoration of balance and manageability in her life and that of the family.

Case study for identification purposes

The purpose of the case study is to assist you, the reader, to identify the stages through which Miriam has travelled on her journey to change, while assisting you in identifying the stages on your own journey of personal change.

Miriam and the Livingwheel[©]*System*

Case study 3

The issue for Miriam spans many years. She married at the tender age of 20, and before she knew it she was a mother of a young son named John. She had known her husband Henry for many years and loved him dearly. However, over the years and indeed after their marriage, he began to drink heavily while she was left to mind and care for their son, as well as many other household activities.

As Miriam was unemployed she was dependent and relied very much on Henry. She relied on him to keep the household running smoothly as Henry was the controller of the household budget, paying for food, clothing, mortgage and the usual household utilities.

As his drinking descended into an uncontrollable and downwards spiral, Miriam became more and more despondent and feared for the loss of their home, as payments that otherwise should have been given towards their home and upkeep of the family were now going down the drain, literally, by way of alcohol consumption.

These events resulted in many domestic arguments and broken promises. However, these words were not to change Henry as he was in the throes of alcoholism and it had generated a selfish life of its own. There were days when all seemed well without alcohol being present in the relationship, only to disintegrate a day or two later into an uncontrollable spiral of drinking and domestic violence.

These broken promises, disappointments and hurt eventually began to take their toll on Miriam. She was also very concerned about the environment that her son John, now seven months old, was in the midst of. She visited her doctor who prescribed for her medication for anxiety as she was not able to cope very well with the demands of a new baby for the past seven months. However, Miriam never explained to him about her domestic situation and the affair her husband

Henry was having with 'Lady Booze.'

Miriam's emotional and mental health were affected by Henry's behaviour and she knew it. But after all, if she left their home with her son John, where would she go? She had no money as Henry now controlled every penny to keep his addiction in place. She was penniless, heartbroken, emotionally and mentally unwell and full of despair.

She would stay awake at nights waiting to hear the door open just so as she would know that Henry was home. She feared secretly he would be killed or kill someone while driving from his second home, the pub, to his family home. The home he was in the process of wrecking as well as the lives of those nearest and dearest to him.

What am I going to do? she repeatedly asked herself, dependent, hurt, penniless, heartbroken and with feelings of shame and isolation. These were some of the effects that alcoholism was having on her and her son, John. She was in the depths of despair and began to feel that God had abandoned her and was in some way punishing her for whatever reason. She had had enough. She felt beaten and alone and needed to do something but unsure of what it was she needed to do.

However it was during a visit to the doctor's surgery as John was now nine months old and had gotten a chest infection, that she noticed a poster on the surgery wall saying in big print, "Are you affected by someone else's drinking?". The sign seemed to jump out at her and speak to her directly shouting at her to take notice. Yet, this was happening in the relative quiet of the surgery waiting room.

The contact number and details seemed huge as she stared at them as though in silent conversation with them, while at the same time memorising the name, contact person and contact details. It was at this point everything in the room seemed silent except for this poster screaming at her, as she gulped for air while her heart was pounding in her chest. Was this the answer to her long awaited prayers?

Miriam noticed at the bottom of the poster there were pieces of paper with a number on them. As the seconds ticked by, she was torn. Will I? Won't I? Who will see me? She was fearful that her name would be called next. Miriam walked over to the poster, her palms were sweating and her mouth was dry. With baby John in her arms Miriam pretended to show him some children's pictures on the wall as she secretly and very quickly tore off a contact strip containing the information from the poster and swiftly shoved it into her pocket.

Miriam hoped nobody had seen her in the process. With that, the secretary called her name and she walked with John in her arms into the awaiting doctor as though nothing had happened. But it had! Something very big had just taken place. A personal and intimate moment between the universe and Miriam. She had been offered a way forward. The universe had come to her rescue and had offered her a choice and what's more, perhaps even the direction to take.

During the visit Miriam was physically present to the doctor and her baby son John, however mentally she was in a different space altogether. Her head was racing with thoughts of what had just happened and she couldn't wait to leave the surgery with John. She was experiencing a state of shock and disbelief and yet deep inside her she knew what it was she had to do. Yes, get home and make that all important phone call which she repeatedly checked upon ensuring it was still in her pocket. Miriam eventually left the surgery, located her car and drove to her home. On arrival home she was feeling anxious, nervous entering into a house where symbolically there was a smiley face on the front door and on the inside a face of sorrow, depression and tears. A mask and/or charade Miriam had portrayed for many years to the outside world, and more importantly, to herself.

A house with a story that no one had known or at least she thought and hoped no one had known about, as she had managed to keep the secret from the outside world for a long time by way of denial cover-up and games. By this time she was really good at playing games in keeping her secret a secret.

After attending to the needs of baby John she pondered, paused and hesitated. Was she doing the right thing? Was it really all that bad? Or was she exaggerating and making something big out of nothing? After all, she had seen and heard people talk on TV about these issues and they seemed to have coped well under the circumstances. Was she betraying her husband? Didn't her vows of marriage say, "For better or for worse"? She had made her bed and now she would have to lie in it. Miriam's head was racing again, only this time with hesitancy. She had endured Henry's behaviour up and until now. Perhaps he might change in the near future and all would be well in the marriage and their relationship. However, he would have to stop drinking for this to happen. Again, Miriam found herself caught between "Will I" and "Won't I".

Her mind flashed back to the surgery and the vision of the poster on the wall. How long has it been there she asked herself? Why have I not seen it before? Why should I see it today, above all days? Intuitively at some level Miriam knew that she had to make the call. She placed her hand in her pocket, took the paper in her hand, and looked at it. What if she knows me and Henry? What if it is a neighbour? What if it costs money? Dear God, what am I going to do?

Miriam walked towards the phone which was situated in her sitting room. It was and seemed like the longest walk she ever had to make. She placed her hand on the phone and dialled the number which she had placed on the table beside the phone. As she dialled the number she was feeling anxious and nervous, her hand was trembling. Having dialled the last digit she waited. The phone at the other end began ringing. On the third or fourth ring a lady answered and said: "Good morning, my name is Jacinta. How can I help you?" Her voice sounded calm and peaceful and much older than that of Miriam's.

Miriam described how she had gotten the number and began to explain the difficulties she was experiencing. There was complete quiet from Jacinta as she listened intensely, allowing Miriam the opportunity to explain the difficulties she was experiencing. This one phone call was the beginning of change in Miriam's life as she arranged to meet Jacinta for coffee and explain the workings of a support group for those affected by someone else's alcoholism.

Over the next number of weeks Jacinta and Miriam kept in touch speaking to each other at least once per day. Miriam began to learn about alcoholism and its effects on the family. She began to reach an understanding that it was a disease and not the persons fault. She also learned that some people are of the belief that alcoholism is genetic and incurable, even sometimes fatal, but manageable by way of abstinence.

She also came to the understanding that it was not her fault and that she had done nothing wrong. That she didn't cause it, she couldn't cure it and she certainly couldn't control it but was affected by it. Miriam eventually joined the local support group and met with other men and women who were experiencing similar issues resulting from a family member whose drinking was out of control. The group also helped her to gain acceptance that she had her own life to live, that she had no control over her husband's behaviour, but she had control over the effects of his behaviour on her.

Miriam now had an outlet of support and understanding with people who were in some way intrinsically connected by way of a debilitating disease known as alcoholism. Eight months of support and guidance later Miriam has had time to reflect on the events of her life, including those in her own family and her hidden fears of rejection and abandonment. It was a long journey of emotional turmoil, fear, uncertainty and insecurity.

However Miriam is now in a space where she has the support, guidance and experience of others to help her on her path through life. Baby John is 17 months old and is walking and talking his way through his own young life. Henry, on the other hand, has been hospitalised on two occasions as a result of his alcoholism and is currently in a treatment centre grasping at sobriety yet again. It was during one of the support group meetings, while Miriam was talking with a friend, he made mention of a system which he uses, called the Livingwheel System. He had attended one of the workshops and found the tool and system very useful in his life, and that he would give to her the information at the next meeting.

At the next support group meeting, as promised, he gave Miriam the information and book, which contained the website, email and contact number of the facilitator. Miriam made contact with him and arranged to attend one of the forthcoming workshops. She is now incorporating the tool and system, assisting her manageability with issues of concern in her life

MY LAW TIEME RANAPIRI

The sun may be clouded, but ever the sun,

Will sweep on its course till the cycle is run, And when into chaos the system is hurled,

Again shall the builder, rebuild a new world.

Your path may be clouded, uncertain your goal,

Move on, for your orbit is fixed to your soul, And though may it lead you through darkness of night,

The torch of the Builder shall give it new light.

You were, you will be,

Know this while you are,

Your spirit has travelled both long and afar. It rose from the source, to the Source it returns, the spark which was lighted eternally burns.

It slept in a jewel, it leapt in a wave,

It roamed in a forest, it rose from the grave.

MATTHEW HALLIGAN

It took on strange garbs for long eons of years, And now in the soul of yourself it appears.

From body to body your spirit speeds on,

It seeks a new form when the old one has gone. And the form that it finds is the fabric you wrought,

On the loom of the mind from the fibre of thought.

As dew is drawn upwards in rain to descend, Your thoughts drift away and in destiny blend.

You cannot escape them, for petty or great,

Or evil or noble, they fashion your fate. Somewhere on this planet, sometime and somehow,

Your life is reflecting your thoughts of your NOW!

My law is unerring, no blood can atone,

The structure you built, you will live in alone.

From cycle to cycle, through time and through space,

Your lives with your longings will ever keep pace.

And all that you ask for and all you desire, Must come at your bidding, as flame out of fire. Once list' to that voice and all tumult is done, Your life is the life of the infinite one.

In the hurrying race, you are conscious of pause,

With love for the purpose and love for the cause.

You are your own devil, you are your own God,

You fashioned the paths that your footsteps have trod.

And NOTHING, will save you from error or sin,

Until you have harked to the Spirit within.

(Attributed to the Maori)

ABOUT THE AUTHOR

 Having been employed by a communications company as a technician, the last seven years of which entailed presentations, information technology tutoring and photography, I took early retirement in April 2000 at the age of 47. In 2003 while visiting a friend in a rehabilitation centre, I was to see an advertisement for a diploma course in addiction counselling. I was accepted into the course and graduated two years later. In 2005 I was responsible for the creation of the Better Life Centre, which subsequently evolved into the Open Door Centre, in Mullingar County Westmeath, Ireland. Since 2005 I have worked in the area of addiction, personal assertiveness and group facilitation, comprising of awareness, recovery and change, incorporating communication as the accommodating factor.

My qualifications include a Diploma in Addiction Counselling, Certificate in Psychology, life coach, Train the Trainer and a Distinction in Photography from the Irish Photographic Federation. I have journeyed the Camino on five occasions. A medieval pilgrimage to Santiago De Compostela, in Northwestern Spain. My first Camino took place in July 1996. I experienced alcoholism for 25 years and now enjoy many days of sobriety. I am divorced and have remarried. I remarried in July 2005 to my spiritual partner Mary and have a daughter Alexandra, aged 13 years. I also have four sons from my previous marriage. My wife Mary has two children from a previous marriage. I met Mary on the 9th April 1992. Alexandra is our seventh child born in 1999, in the seventh year of our relationship.

In February 2012 I became unemployed, which gave me the opportunity to develop and expand the Livingwheel System for managing change which I created in 2009. My intention is to deliver training courses and workshops on the

Livingwheel System as a tool which I believe can assist people to restore realignment and balance in their lives by way of embracing change. I live in Northwest Donegal overlooking the Atlantic Ocean and enjoy a deep feeling of belonging and purpose. I enjoy classical music and have a wonderful Labrador retriever called "Fatzo".

Speaking of which (animals that is), I have my favourites with which I can identify mostly with.

They include the Humpback whale, my symbol of communication and depth. The cheetah, my symbol of speed and agility. The eagle, for its ability to view from above and see the larger picture. The hawk, for its ability to remain still and focused, and of course, the turtle, for when I feel the need to retreat into my shell and take time out from life, only to re-emerge into the outside world when I feel that it is safe to do so.

The pheasant, who doesn't fear showing his true colours but is also aware of when not to show them, as remaining camouflaged is its natural protection of reducing the risks of exposure and vulnerability. The butterfly, my personal symbol of change, and of course my camera, a tool which facilitates me in expressing and sharing the beauty of what I witness in nature, as a projection of the divine. Each of the elements within and belonging to our cosmic family, expressing themselves by way of light, colour, shape and appearance, in their own unique, individual and characteristic way from their Source, the creator.

FINALLY

Should you require further information concerning the workings of Livingwheel System for managing change or would like to attend one of my workshops, I can be contacted via the following:

Email:livingwheel@gmail.com

Facebook: www.facebook.com/livingwheel

Web: www.livingwheelcoaching.com

Phone: 00353876395236

Thanking You

Matthew

NOTES

NOTES

NOTES

NOTES

NOTES

Lightning Source UK Ltd.
Milton Keynes UK
UKHW011119151021
392259UK00001B/41